instant
HAPPY

10-second attitude makeovers

KAREN SALMANSOHN

best-selling author of *How to Be Happy, Dammit*

TEN SPEED PRESS
Berkeley

acknowledgments

Humongous thanks to my two wonderful guys, Ari and Howard, for being such inspiring muses—morning, noon, and night. (And sometimes inspiring me to create a poster at 5 a.m.!)

Super-sized appreciation to my go-to support team: Gloria Salmansohn, Marcia Bronstein, Eric Salmansohn, Lia Salmansohn, Ross Salmansohn, Mary Beth Leonard, Lisa Attea, Donna Sonkin, Karen Giberson, Denise Barry, Jennifer Pastiloff, Danielle Pashko, Josselyne Herman, Natalia Petrzela, Susan Shapiro, Hyleri Katzenberg, Marie Forleo, Christi Smith Scoffield, Lalita Khosla, Lindsay Kriger, Dodinsky, Doe Zantamata, Lisa Blecker, David Maleh, Murray Hidary, Nigel Austin, Peter Winick, Richard Kastleman, Kizia Kastleman, Jay Weiss, Michael Simon, Rob Weiss, David Hepworth, Kyle Wilson, Jim Pinkenberg, BJ Gallagher, Eric Zentner, Jen Groover, Alexis Wolfer, Jonathan Fields, Gretchen Rubin, Heidi Krupp, Eric Handler, Keith Ferrazzi, Goldie Hawn, and Peter Guber.

Venti-sized gratitude to the amazing powerhouse behind this book: Emily Timberlake, Rebecca Gradinger, Lisa Westmoreland, Betsy Stromberg, Kara Van De Water, and Elisabeth Beller.

Tidal waves of love for the awesome people who come to my daily blog at www.notsalmon.com and my Facebook fan page, and for all the wonderful members of my *Be Happy, Dammit* newsletter! Thank you all for cheering me on with your loving notes and inspiring stories of resilience!

introduction

Want to be happy, dammit? If so, you gotta teach your old brain some new tricks and start thinking more optimistically! When you train your brain to think more positive thoughts, you're more likely to form positive habits—which then leads you to more positive results. (And I'm positive about that!)

Unfortunately, it's not always easy to think positively. Life is full of ups and downs; it ebbs and flows. And sometimes during the tough times, we find ourselves stuck in a downward "negative-thought spiral." All too quickly we go from thinking "this one thing sucks" to "my whole DAY sucks" to "my WHOLE LIFE sucks" to "THE WORLD SUCKS" to "DISTANT GALAXIES SUCK!"

So, what's the solution? ***Instant Happy***, of course! This book uses a psychological tool called **pattern interrupts** to stop a moving train of negative thoughts in its tracks. Each page in this book offers a different pattern interrupt—or what I refer to as a **"happy-thought intervention"**—designed to counteract limiting beliefs and jumpstart a new pattern of positive, productive thought.

But what's the big deal with positivity, anyway? Well, in order to answer that question, we first have to look at what's so wrong with negative thinking.

Neuroscientists have a biological explanation for why those downward negative-thought spirals happen in the first place. MRIs have shown that every time people think angry thoughts or imagine worst-case scenarios, they send a surge of blood flowing into the brain regions associated with depression and anger—which *refuels* their depression and anger in a destructive feedback loop. The sadder and angrier you become, the more your body gets flooded with troublemaking "fight or flight" neurochemicals, which shut down the more evolved neocortex part of your brain. Basically, when you're trapped in a really negative fight-or-flight thought pattern, you're limited to using a mere 20 percent of your brain's thinking power. This is why during tough times you might find it very difficult to interpret events correctly, communicate feelings effectively, or think with a long-term optimistic lens.

Happily, MRIs have also shown that when people start to think *happy* thoughts, they send a surge of blood flowing into brain regions associated with happiness—widening their positive neural pathways and making it easier and more automatic for them to think better, calmer thoughts. Meaning? If you keep reading *Instant Happy*, and keep focusing on those happy thought interventions, then over time it will become easier and easier for you to think more positively!

Kind of cool, isn't it—how you can create a happier reality simply by *thinking* in a happier way? Happiness truly does not come from the things you have. It comes from the *thoughts* you have!

So, here's how you can use *Instant Happy* to boost your joy and peace of mind: Whenever you find yourself stuck in a limiting thought pattern, unstick thyself by flipping to a page, any page, in this book. What you'll find is an **inspirational flashcard**—a positive, affirming statement paired with a graphic. (Oh, and about those graphics: Research has shown that when you incorporate visuals into your learning process, you are better at "recording" lessons in your permanent memory bank. So the illustrations in *Instant Happy* aren't just fun to look at—they're also an important tool that will encourage your brain to fully remember all the positive messages it is learning!) You don't have to wait until you're in a bad mood to read these inspirational flashcards. Make a practice of starting or ending your day by reading one of 'em—or two of 'em—or five—or twenty-seven of 'em!

As you're first reading through *Instant Happy*, you may find yourself rejecting many of the positive affirmations because they conflict too much with your current, negative beliefs. Good! The inspirational flashcards that stir up the most resistance are the ones you should pay the most attention to—because they're *definitely* creating a pattern interrupt. Keep rereading these in particular! And remember—even if at first you have to fake the positivity, eventually you will make the positivity. After all, repetition works, repetition works, repetition works!

It may seem hard to believe, but you think 60,000 thoughts a day. The purpose *of Instant Happy* is to give you the tools and the motivation to *choose* happy thoughts—not to waste 59,999 on negative, limited thinking. No matter how busy or stressed you think you are, you always have time for a quick pattern interrupt—think of it as a ten-second attitude makeover! My hope for you is that over time, you'll get closer and closer to your goal of 60,000 positive thoughts a day.

XO
Karen

Think of yourself as being
NEGATIVE-THOUGHT
INTOLERANT.

Just as drinking dairy is bad for the lactose intolerant,

thinking negatively is BAD FOR YOU!

True happiness isn't about the **THINGS** you have; it's about the **THOUGHTS** you have. That's why it's called positive *THINKING* **NOT** positive *THING-ING*.

LOOK FOR 'EM!

Even
bad days
have happy
moments.

When one door closes,
TRY A WINDOW.

**THEN TRY
A NEW DOOR.**

Then try a new window.

The world is full of
doors and windows.

Eventually you'll find one
that stays open.

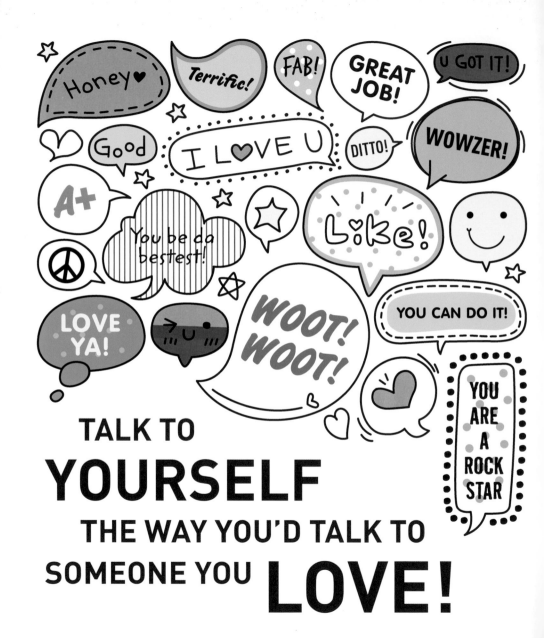

TALK TO **YOURSELF** THE WAY YOU'D TALK TO SOMEONE YOU **LOVE!**

You are wonderful.

Worthwhile.

Loveable.

Not because others think so.

**Self-worth comes from
only one place—**

yourself.

If only I had . . .
If only I didn't have . . .
I can't until . . .
But I'm not . . .
If my family wasn't . . .
Not until . . .
If I don't have . . .
Yes, but . . .
If only I were . . .
If only I weren't . . .
Not now because . . .

WHAT'S YOUR PET EXCUSE?

Isn't it time to set it free?

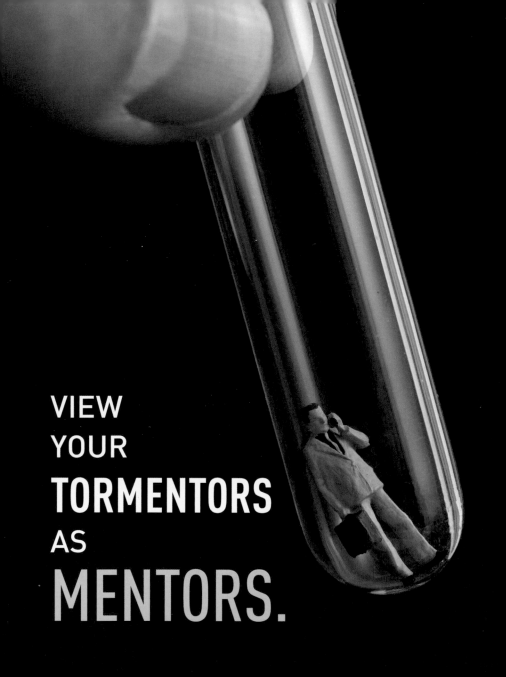

ASK YOURSELF,
"WHAT IS THIS PERSON MEANT TO TEACH ME?"

EVERY PERSON IN OUR LIVES HAS
A LESSON TO TEACH.

SOME LESSONS INCLUDE:

How to be stronger

How to be more communicative

When to trust your intuition

How to be more self-loving

When to let go

Why you want to be nothing
like this person

ANGRY THOUGHTS MAKE YOUR MIND MESSY!

When you stop chasing
the wrong things,

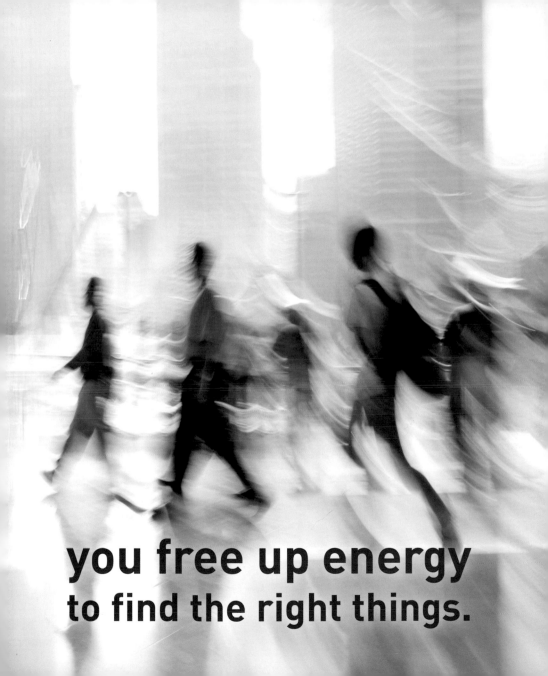

you free up energy
to find the right things.

oy
=
joy

**REFRAME
THE STORIES OF
YOUR LIFE.**

*failure
=
wisdom*

Everything you've ever done, every person you've ever met, every experience you've ever had is a part of who you are today. • Everything you've ever needed to be as it was, otherwise you wouldn't have grown into you.

Accept
what was
and
what is ...

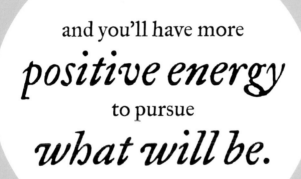

and you'll have more

positive energy

to pursue

what will be.

Repeat after me:
I forgive myself
for not being perfect.

And I recognize none of us are perfect,
so I am open to forgiving others.

You know you're
making progress
when you start
making new mistakes.

BEING **AWESOME** IS THE **BEST** **REVENGE.**

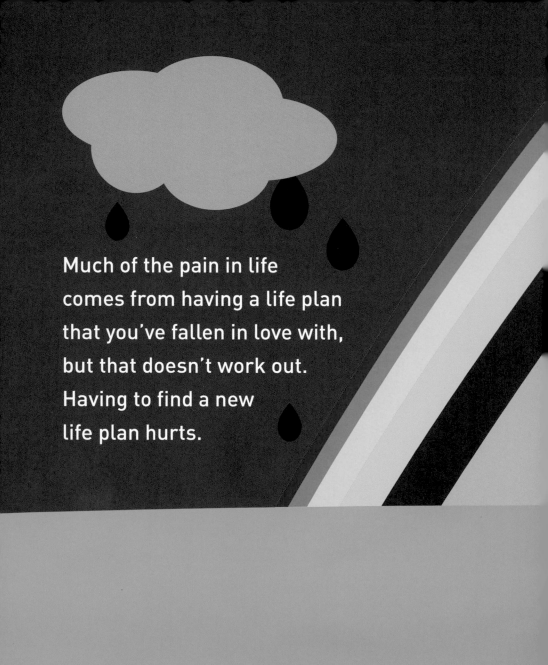

Much of the pain in life
comes from having a life plan
that you've fallen in love with,
but that doesn't work out.
Having to find a new
life plan hurts.

The trick is not to become
too attached to any particular
life plan and to remember
that there is always a better,

EVEN-HAPPIER

life plan out there somewhere.

**Swap
your
"KICK-ME"
sign . . .**

When you feel the weight of the world on your shoulders, think of yourself as a soul builder, strengthening untapped parts of your spirit, growing into your best, most powerful you!

If you want to be sad,
live in the PAST.

If you want to be anxious,
live in the FUTURE.

If you want
to be peaceful,
live in the
NOW.

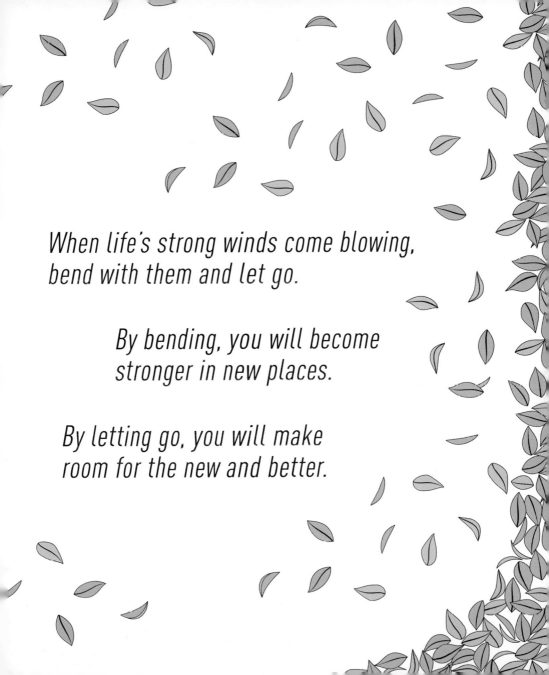

When life's strong winds come blowing,
bend with them and let go.

By bending, you will become
stronger in new places.

By letting go, you will make
room for the new and better.

Don't
look
back*

*unless it's
to catch
the gaze of
an admirer.

When life
starts feeling
a bit
too serious,
find someone
you can
GIGGLE with!

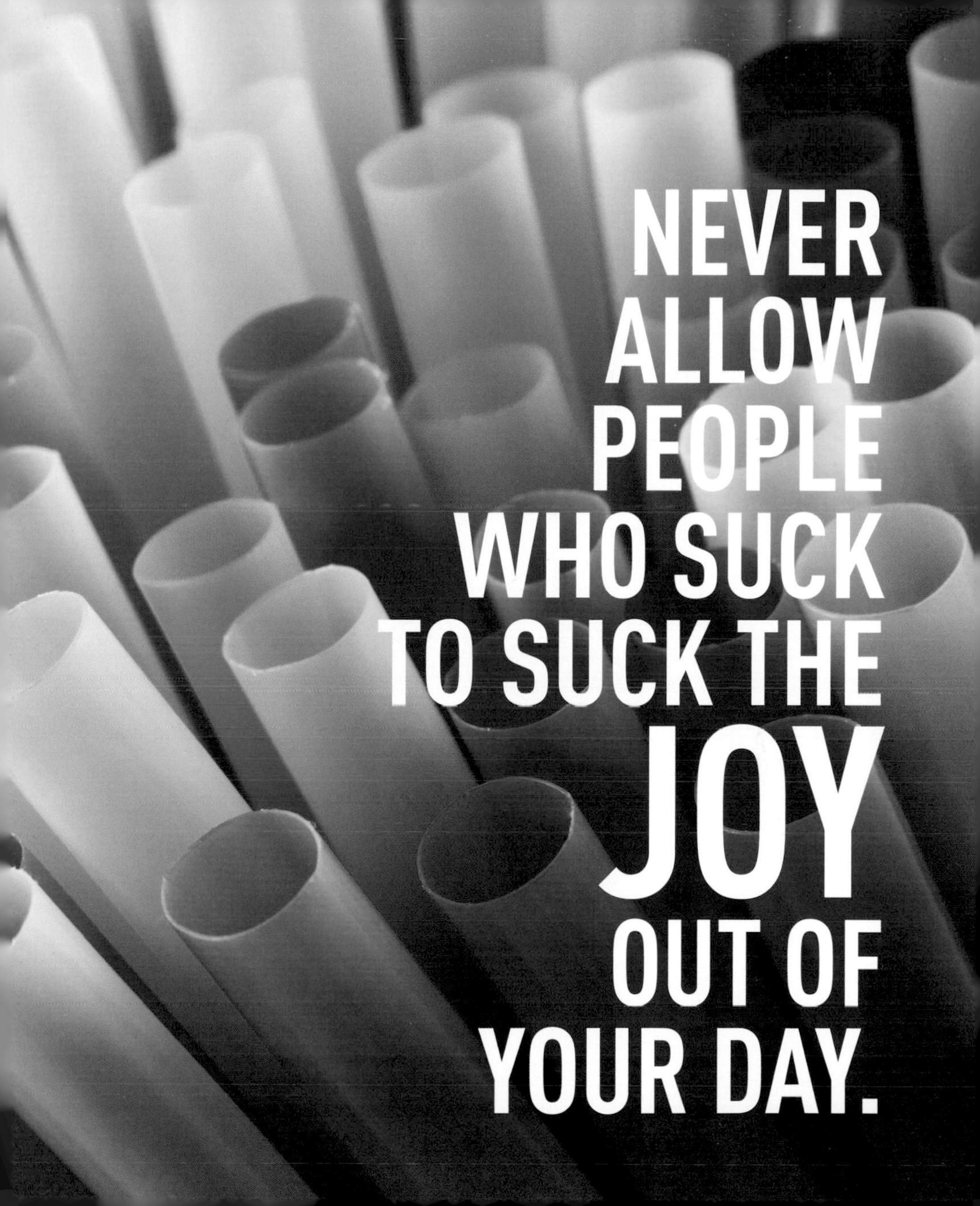

NEVER
ALLOW
PEOPLE
WHO SUCK
TO SUCK THE
JOY
OUT OF
YOUR DAY.

Every day is a new
opportunity to change your life.
You have the power to say
"This is not how my story ends."

You have the power to rewrite your destiny.

The wisest guru
is your inner you.

DON'T LET
A BAD DAY

**make you
feel like
you have
a bad life.**

We're all beautifully different.

Cherish what makes you
you.

Certificate
of
Self-Worth

YOU ARE WORTHY OF
Asking.

YOU ARE WORTHY OF
Getting.

Know the difference between
FAKE FRIENDS and **TRUE FRIENDS.**

A true friend is there for you
when you need 'em—
and even when you say
you don't need 'em . . .

but really kinda do.

Trees that endure the stormiest times grow to be the STRONGEST and MOST BEAUTIFUL.

Ditto how your stormy times can encourage you to thrive and **BLOOM INTO YOUR MIGHTIEST YOU.**

*Don't let yesterday's bad times
or bad feelings influence
today's thoughts and mood.*

You shouldn't choose
to dress for
yesterday's rain
if there are
sunny skies today.

IF
YOU
CAN
READ
THIS

you have many reasons to be grateful!

You're alive.
You can read.
You have access to books.

No matter how challenging
your life may feel,
see your life clearly.

FOCUS ON THE
MANY THINGS YOU HAVE
TO BE GRATEFUL FOR!

When in the midst of CHAOS,

find that
STILLNESS
within you.

Get curious, not furious.

ASK YOURSELF:

What else can this mean?

How might this be a good thing in disguise?

To hell with always being an early bird.

Sometimes when you catch some zzzz's, you are more capable of catching that worm.

GO ON A "NO NUTS" DIET.

AVOID PEOPLE WHO DRIVE YOU NUTS.

WAVE GOODBYE TO STRESS
BY ENVISIONING YOUR MIND AS
OCEAN WAVES.

QUIET YOUR MIND
BY ENVISIONING THE WATER GETTING
QUIETER AND QUIETER

UNTIL THERE'S
NOT EVEN
A RIPPLE ON ITS SURFACE.

Sometimes you must accept
when something is truly broken.

If you try to fix it,
you can get hurt.

Instead of hoping to make it better,
choose to create something better.

The sooner you let go
of what's broken,
the sooner you can

BEGIN ANEW.

Complaining is draining!

Commit to talking 20% about the problem and 80% about the solution.

Soon, complaining will seem **100%** boring!

Worry not only
DISTRACTS, it
ATTRACTS.

It can become an
accidental magnet
for the things
you do not want.

LOVE IS A DRUG.

USE IT
RESPONSIBLY.

Perform random acts of love daily.

WARNING:

When you fall for someone with all your heart,

remember to take your head with you.

When someone leaves you,
let them go.

*Their part in the story
of your life may be over,
but your story goes on.*

More important than surrounding
yourself with LOTS of people . . .

is finding a handful of people
who support you LOTS!

GOOD
LOOKS
FADE.

But a good heart
keeps you beautiful
forever.

Who's
in favor
of finding
as many
reasons
as possible
to purr
with happiness
today?

"SEXY"
ISN'T ABOUT
WHAT YOU WEAR.

IT'S ABOUT HOW YOU FEEL.

The more passion you feel
for yourself and your life,
the more passion
others will feel for you.

View your life with
KINDSIGHT.

Stop beating yourself up about things from your past.

Instead of slapping your forehead and asking,
"WHAT WAS I THINKING?"
breathe and ask the kinder question,
"WHAT WAS I LEARNING?"

The best
things
happen at the
exit ramp

from your
comfort zone.

When you **STOP WASTING ENERGY** on worry and fear, it's like removing emotional static from your mind and getting a cable hookup to the rest of the world.

Not only is the picture
of your life clearer;
YOU HAVE MORE
VIEWING OPTIONS.

So don't be afraid to
fly to new heights;
just spread your wings and
TRY.

Coffee

+

Positivity

=

An Unstoppable Duo

HOCUS FOCUS:

What you think about
is what you attract.

So fill your mind with

PEACE, JOY,

LOVE, and

STRENGTH,

and your life will reflect
what you're thinking of!

YOU GOTTA

FAITH IT

TO

MAKE IT!

LOOKING FOR A MIRACLE TO HAPPEN?

Consider that perhaps something *not* happening was your miracle.

If a goal or dream is slow in coming, envision it on a delivery truck,

just a wee bit stuck in traffic,
but still headed toward you.

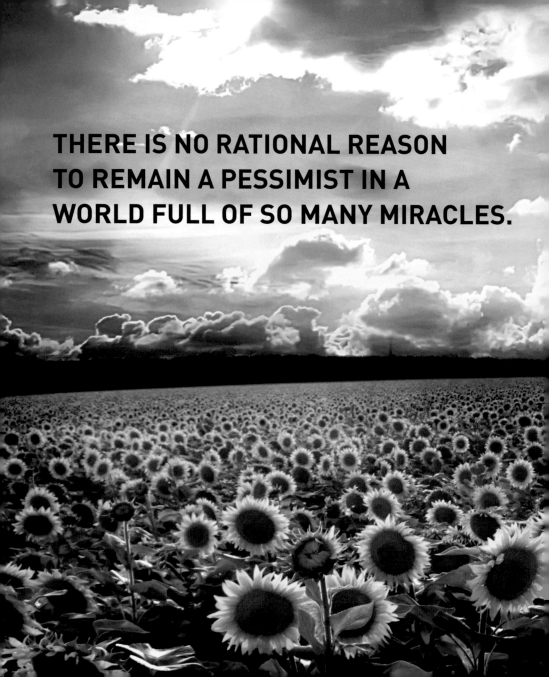

GO FOR YOUR DREAMS.

(DON'T BE A WUSS.)

Don't let people who
never pursued their dreams try to
talk you out of pursuing yours.

SPOILER ALERT:

IT WILL ALL WORK OUT FOR YOU IN THE END.

Library of Congress Cataloging-in-Publication Data
Salmansohn, Karen.
  Instant happy : 10-second attitude makeovers / Karen Salmansohn.
    p. cm.
  1. Happiness. 2. Attitude (Psychology) 3. Optimism. I. Title.
BF575.H27S342 2012
158.1—dc23
                    2012012083

ISBN 978-1-60774-368-2
eISBN 978-1-60774-369-9

Printed in China

Book design by Betsy Stromberg

10 9 8

First Edition